Ghost Heart

Winner of the Sixth Annual
Ex Ophidia Press Prize for Poetry
2021

Ex Ophidia Press

Praise for Mary Pinard's *Portal*

In *Portal,* Mary Pinard explores grief and its transformations — both agonizing and transcendent — with a range and skill that are breathtaking. Here, the portal in its many manifestations (window, aperture, lens, doorway, insight) becomes both obstruction and passage, that which at once separates us from what we most desire and gives us access. Along the way, Pinard's powerful, lovely, and sometimes horrific imaginings and figurings evoke and invoke our own deepest fears and loves. This is an enormously brave, tough book, compelling and beautiful, a tour-de-force.

— Katharine Coles

Grief has the power to shatter or transform us. Mary Pinard is a visionary who dares to dive into the wreck, exploring the deepest realms of human consciousness and surfacing with gorgeously wrought revelations of what it means to survive, to love, to continue. She speaks to the lost in voices no longer personal: wind and water, sweetgrass and diesel engine, salmonid and sand eel. With transcendent tenderness, *Portal* opens a window on a world of radiant wonder.

— Melanie Rae Thon

Mary Pinard's book *Portal* consists of a number of poems recounting the circumstances of her brother's death, drowned in the kitchen galley of a capsized tugboat; the poems are heartbreakingly and unsentimentally a catalogue of the circumstances, what kind of person her dead brother was, and what have been the consequences, meditative cataloguing, too, of her own feelings of bereavement. The poems, for the most part in free-verse, are highly controlled, in a wide variety of dignified and deeply expressive forms rhythmically proceeding in their telling of the story. Separate poems, each beautiful in itself, but, taken together, it is one poem, in my opinion a great poem, a great elegiac poem.

— David Ferry

Ghost Heart

Poems

Mary Pinard

Ex Ophidia Press
2022

First edition.
Manufactured in the United States of America.

James T. Jones, Publisher.
Richard-Gabriel Rummonds, Publisher Emeritus.
Sharon Cumberland, Director of the Poetry Book Prize Contest.
Kathleen Flenniken, judge of the 2021 contest.
Ex Ophidia Press advisory board: Sheila Bender, Abby Murray, and Gregory Richter.
John D. Wagner, public relations and marketing.

Cover painting by Lisa Grossman.
Open Range Burn,
Watercolor on paper, 2.5 x 9.5 inches,
© 2001
Production: Fabio Laniado.
Publication acknowledgements are listed on page 98.

Published by Ex Ophidia Press
17037 10th Avenue NE
Shoreline, WA 98155
exophidiapress.org

ISBN: 978-1-7373851-4-1

Always, Miles

Contents

/////

I. A Prairie Georgic

/////

II. A Mending

Ghost Heart

form from form from form from form

— Ronald Johnson, *ARK*

I was making language
a stem to aspire to :

durable   flexible   able
to register shift quickly—

when shaken
to keep shape.

— Brian Teare, *Companion Grasses*

What Will Happen

                    to this
carved out place, once
rough and undisturbed, now
fallen, sparse, already
a remnant from lives
lost to the inexorable? Who
will care that such care was
taken to choose for this path
limestone, of the type layered
with traces of an ancient winding
river, rather than one pocked with fossil
remains in bands of buff clay? Or that
this fence-line transected a prairie
parcel here, or that this mix of mineral
supplements for beef cattle was blended
to satisfy this percentage instead of that? Who
will burn the invasive hedge, cedar, smooth
brome, the buckthorn? Who will remember
which of these hills hold burial mounds for the Kansa,
Wichita, Pawnee? Who will keep the skeleton
key for the district common school,
a replica, open it for tours? Who will
make the time to deadhead the fading
wild irises, keep the open range
road graded, the bison skull hanging
on the barn from slipping
off its nail?

/////

I. A Prairie Georgic

And someday, in those fields the crooked plow
Of a farmer laboring there will turn up a spear,
Almost eaten away with rust, or his heavy hoe
Will bump against an empty helmet, and
He'll wonder at the giant bones in that graveyard.

— Virgil, *The Georgics*

I never got to tell you about that first time
I ever walked on a prairie without you, which was
of course by then already a remnant. The word
widow new to me and strange, I was at a conference
about how to begin to rebuild this eco-system,
over time so damaged that it's now scattered,
like the small tatters and trimmings of quilting fabric
fallen on the floor around my sewing machine, here,
there, remembrances. That day, I was part of a field
trip, a novice in the company of plant biologists, local
botanists, microbiologists, and prairie restorationists.
Once we were walking, slowly, slowly, in the dense
weave of grasses and forbs, they didn't really talk
to each other as much as sing, madrigal-like, as they
called out, and called out the species they were
seeing — *Dalea candida, Lespedeza capitata,*
Silphium laciniatum, Asclepias tuberosa, Mimosa
nuttallii, Spartina pectinata, Bouteloua gracilis.
I listened, feeling myself becoming

    Big bluestem, Needle-
    and-Thread, Indian, Buffa-
    lo, Sweet, Switch, Dropseed.

It was
  itself, abundance,
     a vast
        skin, living

     echo-system of climate, flux
  of matter, and energy. As in a solar system, or
     ocean, or span of geologic time, it was perspective
 and its loss,

     inevitable erasures. It was
   itself still
    ungraspable in its spatial
      scale, its horizons, its strata.

    Nearly half of it was
     underground.

It is
  the vulture, dark, elegant-winged
      just
lifting off a dusty county road in mid-summer, and in its beak a large black snake —

the long body stiff, yet recurring in curves, as if its final moments
   were hurriedly written, a line in long-
  hand from memory, before being
    carried, now

      carried up, into.

It has been
already for ages the detritus of a succession —
inland seas, seizings, their coming-and-going rhythms
encompassing,

shallow, a translucent covering
about 70 million years ago of

most of Central North America, in direct response — a call-and-response
matter — to ice pack and ice caps (they were big enough to make
their own climate),
pulled and turned, folded and

shelved by cooling and warming, the vicissitudes
of weather, always in some relationship to one, or

the other. At the coldest, most complete
glaciation, so much
of the planet's water was locked up
in continental ice sheets
that the worldwide sea level was hundreds of feet less than

                                        it is now. But once the
                gradual

        warming   held,
                                    and held,
                it shrunk the vast ice,
                                        and so the once ice-bound

    and buried hills, valleys, ridges, slopes,
                                and hollows emerged,
            and the lakes and rivers
                    coursed,

                        of course also reshaping
                                        what had been.

Such a profound departure,
          (what was the sound
                    of that heavy gouging?) that left,
between the western
                    and eastern forests,
                    and in the rain shadow
          of the western mountains —
          a laying down, and
                    down again, a leaving
                         of impressions pressed into
                    the mud, the silt of the drying sea bottom that then
          hardening into shale, held

     the former sea's embeddings, fossils:
                              leaves, twigs, fronds
                              of kelp, the miscellaneous
                                   worms, jellyfish,
                    sponges,
                    the clamlike, the primitive
          relatives   of sea stars,
               and ripple marks,
     and undulations,
               notations in the strata.
                                   Testimonials.
          And eventually
                    spearheads   of the first immigrants,
                    hunters crossing the Bering
                              land bridge, or
having to skirt the remaining retreating glaciers in skin boats, moving
          30,000 years ago south along the coast,
               themselves, and their beloveds
                         floating on the long waving arms
               of kelp beds.

I saw an erratic on the prairie
        near where I released you,

                your ashes.

How delicate,
            given the scale
                        was the leaving behind also a cleaving
of boulders,
heavy with origin,
                  fugitives,   glacial
                              transports named erratics — from *errare*
to wander.   When seen,
                        oddly placed,
                                    one at the edge of a field

    another in the midst of a woods
                              still another
on a shore,
        on a bluff:
                  each a tracery of its own path,
                                    and the whole of
                  earth's heart.

Grass, isn't it the orphic skin of the prairie, where
weather is meted out by rites of sun, or rain, wind or
fire? The circulatory soil makes and remakes
fossils, holds root systems, tunnels open for unseen
migrations — cells and worms, the long-gone shifting
sea, its markings, maskings. I never got to see it, this

sea-like land early white settlers claimed, an undersky of
grass, that's what they said it looked like, these weary
migrants, living for the first time through the unfamiliar
weather patterns of the prairie. They were not unlike
fossils of the Old World already, finding themselves with
fire that scrolled and unscrolled the horizon. How much

fire, they couldn't have imagined, having only just
seen the sea, and the sea, and the sea so wide before them.
Fossils would have surprised them too but for all that
grass, burned, but growing back, an endless greening seam.
Whether worked by the Cheyenne, Plains, or by climate, it held
migrant traces of older places — bones, limestone, deep-laced

migratory roots, marked by molten journeys from the dark,
fire rivering up and up to the surface. Is it possible to know
whether anyone really wanted to move that far, to have to
see so much that might not have been like home? Like
grass? Who knew there could be such vastness, and that
fossils could be as big as the wagons their oxen pulled,

fossils that still today jut up, walls of chalk left behind by
migrating seas, restless, seized, but ghostly, hardened, like
grasses bleached white by the sun, the shifting chemistry of soil,
fire too with its sculpting blow-throughs, holes that can still be
seen, from afar, like when we drove to see those monuments
weathering off the interstate in western Kansas, and didn't know

whether we'd ever find them, till we came to a herd of pronghorns,
fossils, didn't they seem to be from another age, from when the
sea had just washed through here, leaving in its path the making of
migration mandatory — how movement, under and above the ground
winds it all around us, like some kind of endless rope, a lassoing
grass:

grass, weathering to
fossils in a lonely wind:
we migrants, a sea.

And by the time Zebulon Pike and his expedition crossed
the vast tallgrass prairie of central Kansas, on their way to ex-
plore Colorado, and beyond, the shallow but impatient inland seas had been
writing themselves out, coming and going, coming and going across the bedrock
there for millions of years — some say 250, some 280, some 299 — leaving behind an extra-
ordinary layering, a building up, alluvial, sedimentary, and aeolian, an autobiography of great height,
an alternating alliteration of shale, limestone, strata studded with fossils and flint: hard, insoluble,
edgy, opalescent flint — the same flint used by generations and generations of Pawnee, Osage,
Wichita, and Kansa tribes for arrowheads, and later, much, much later by Revolutionary
colonists in the cocks of their flintlock rifles — flint, a type of quartz, that might
also, some claim, be organic, formed from remains of tiny marine organisms,
diatoms and radiolarians, whose fantastic glass-like bones drifted,
dissolved, then repaired as nodes of flint, and since the final
retreat of the seas, these boney layers have held, resisting
erosions by wind, and weather, and bison, and
almost, the plow.

Version 1

The Indian tribes residing within the limits of the U.S. have for a considerable time been growing more & more uneasy at the constant diminution of the territory they occupy, altho' effected by their own voluntary sales: and the policy has long been gaining strength with them, of refusing absolutely all further sale, on any conditions; insomuch that, at this time, it hazards their friendship, and excites dangerous jealousies and perturbations in their minds to make any overture for the purchase of the smallest portions of their land. A very few tribes only are not yet obstinately in these dispositions. In order peaceably to counteract this policy of theirs, and to provide an extension of territory which the rapid increase of our numbers will call for, two measures are deemed expedient. First, to encourage them to abandon hunting, to apply to the raising stock, to agriculture and domestic manufacture, and thereby prove to themselves that less land & labor will maintain them in this, better than in their former mode of living. The extensive forests necessary in the hunting life will then become useless, & they will see advantage in exchanging them for the means of improving their farms, & of increasing their domestic comforts. Secondly to multiply trading houses among them & place within their reach those things which will contribute more to their domestic comfort, than the possession of extensive, but uncultivated wilds, experience & reflection will develop to them the wisdom of exchanging what they can spare & we want, for what we can spare and they want.

Version 2

The Indian tribes residing within the limits of the U.S. have for a considerable time been growing more & more uneasy at the constant diminution of the territory they occupy, altho' effected by their own voluntary sales: and the policy has long been gaining strength with them, of refusing absolutely all further sale, on any conditions; insomuch that, at this time, it hazards their friendship, and excites dangerous jealousies and perturbations in their minds to make any overture for the purchase of the smallest portions of their land. A very few tribes only are not yet obstinately in these dispositions. In order peaceably to counteract this policy of theirs, and to provide an extension of territory which the rapid increase of our numbers will call for, two measures are deemed expedient. First, to encourage them to abandon hunting, to apply to the raising stock, to agriculture and domestic manufacture, and thereby prove to themselves that less land & labor will maintain them in this, better than in their former mode of living. The extensive forests necessary in the hunting life will then become useless, & they will see advantage in exchanging them for the means of improving their farms, & of increasing their domestic comforts. Secondly to multiply trading houses among them & place within their reach those things which will contribute more to their domestic comfort, than the possession of extensive, but uncultivated wilds, experience & reflection will develop to them the wisdom of exchanging **what** they can spare & **we want**, for what **we** can spare and they **want.**

Deere, John

Settlers recounted that plows cutting through fibrous prairie roots sounded like cloth ripping or the dull roaring of a distant storm, punctuated by a volley of pistol shots as larger tougher roots were severed.

— Cornelia Mutel, *The Emerald Horizon*

It was a shaping age. What wasn't about pushing the point deep in, plunging a curious blade wherever into whatever it could open? Just three months before Lewis and Clark pushed off from St. Louis in 1804, their keelboats and pirogues plying up the Missouri, then roving prairies west by horse and wagon over mountains to the Pacific,
you were born in Vermont on a farm, where your father's tailor shop was your first
world — bolts of fabric, cutting tables, shears, the needles you would have helped polish, sharpen, slipping them again and again in buckets of sand, or bags of emery. That would have taken
long honing. Some said you were entranced, seeing
day after day the way pitchforks moved in haphazard
stacks of hay or clayey sod. What you saw, thought, it
would have taken patience to grind rough edges off those
steel tines, careful insistence, a rhythmic diligence
for digging, that deft returning — again, again,
again — for ease, but also speed. How this
must have shaped your idea years later
in Illinois to cut a mill-saw blade, shape it
to fit over a wood form, what became
the plains breaker they called it, slicer
of the ancient soil-dark net — you
broke the prairies' grip. By now
your name is green enamel on legions
of tractors: *I will never put my name
on a product that does not have in it
the best that is in me.* After you

became mayor of Moline, you lent
your name to public works — water
pipes, streetlights, sidewalks, city
parks — as if you hoped somehow
that what you broke forever below
could be mended above.

So when I saw for the first time

a bison, it was where I had learned it
would be — in a national park set on a restored prairie
somewhere in eastern South Dakota — and I'd gone to see it

there, because while never really thinking about it, I must
have believed that that's where bison lived, had
always lived, and had through that living become

identified with the idea for me of the West — at least the Middle
West — thanks to cowboy movies like *The Plainsman, Cimarron, and Once
Upon a Time in the West* (where I learned most of what I thought

I knew) about it, the vast grasslands where it grazed alongside
horses, cows, clouds, stagecoaches, fences, occasional
saloon towns, and petty thieves, a sheriff, and constant battles

with Indians, and legends (Wyatt, Daniel, Lone, Wild Bill,
Calamity), and also that all this was associated with an imminent
vanishing, I kept hearing about all this going, possibly already having

gone, away, so I began to try and see things that might not be around
forever, even though I'd grown up in the far West, along the northwest coast
of Washington, on Puget Sound, not too far from the San Juan archipelago,

a shredding of islands in the Salish Sea, where the language of that place —
its towns, its lakes, its rivers, its food, its flowers, its trees, its animals, its
art — was already naming as apology, as lament, as elegy for who and what

had been there before, those first peoples and their many thousand-year-old
culture, so by the time I saw for the first time
a bison, I too was already caught up in the longitude

and latitude, that impending
impaling barbed wire
of absence.

Historical Marker: Nebraska 88*

Looking to switch drivers, we turned off Highway 77
in Nebraska, near a shabby sign that read "Historical Marker."
The pot-holed road was overgrown, though mailboxes lined
the ditch, metal flags up. We parked at the end of pavement,
you getting out to stretch, change your shoes, while I leashed
Shiva, and we walked toward where I thought the marker might
be. Along impressions of faint tire tracks leading into the brush,
canopies of old cottonwoods were letting go their white clusters,
jittery fibers afloat just above the ground-weave of stinging nettles,
poison ivy. Still no sign of a sign about what history transpired
there, I was about to turn back when I startled a fawn, who startled
me. We stiffened, stared — even Shiva was still — seconds, minutes,
time so suddenly slow. Until it saw me, did it hear, sense I was
the missing mother returning? And when I wasn't, and was what
I was instead, did it know the danger of my trespass? It was then
that I saw the marker. When I moved toward it, the fawn fled, so fleet
it left no trace. I took a few steps closer, the faint narrative coming
into view about the Pawnee living here once, near *Pa-huk'* Hill,
a scared place to them. Nearby, they made their earthen lodges,
which ended up being, of their kind, the very, very last.

---

* "Before the Pawnee Indians were placed [sic] on a reservation, they located their last earthlodge villages on these nearby bluffs. *Pa-huk'* Hill, one of the five sacred places of the Pawnee, was also here. The villages were occupied from 1850 to 1859 by the Skidi, Tappage and Grand bands led by head chief Petalesharo. The Republican [sic] band lived some distance up stream. The Pawnee once numbered more than 10,000 people [sic] were recorded in history as early as 1541. Often harassed by the Sioux, the [sic] erected sod walls to protect their villages. The Pawnee were friendly toward whites, and some later served as army scouts.

By 1833 the tribe had given up [sic] all of its land north of the Platter [sic] River. General John M. Thayer and O. D. Richardson, representing Territorial Governor Izard, held a conference with the tribe here in 1855. In 1857 the Indians signed the Treaty [sic] of Table Creek, ceding the rest of their land to the whites. In return [sic] they received [sic] a reservation along the Loup River near present-day Genoa. In 1875 the Pawnee moved [sic] south to Indian Territory, ending their settlement in Nebraska."

From Historical Land Mark Council
Hwy. 77, south side of Platte
Dodge County — Marker 88

Warp

— after Hastings, *miniature weaving with wool and cornhusks (8¼ x 7⅞ in.) by Sheila Hicks*

Note: There are roughly 43 corn companies where Hicks grew up in Hastings, Nebraska, a corn-belt city that used to be a mixed-grass prairie.

           Held
        by fine
           warp threads,
   deep red wool — seven
           corn husks, they are like
shuttles, like shuttlecocks, like
           arrowheads, like knives, like
    fine-stringed lyres, like
           fossil fish tissue, like
    wing cases, like dugout
           canoes, like rough
   shrouds, a weaver's map
           back home,
      husk.

Jaw

Corn is the primary US feed grain — around 90 million acres were planted with it in 2019, accounting for 95% of total feed grain. Of the 13.6 billion bushels produced that year, approximately 12 billion were stored.

— US Department of
Agriculture statistics, 2020

The mother of the boy who was suffocated in an avalanche of stored corn inside the silo said she wasn't surprised by the extent of his injuries, but was shocked that the impact had dislocated his jaw.

— *The New York Times*

The contained world of the concrete-walled silo
is meant to store grain — soybeans, wheat, oats, milo,
processed feed and rice — but mostly corn. Bushels
and bushels and bushels of corn. A top hatch opens
for filling by sky-scraping elevators that lift and pour
enormous amounts, while motorized floor augers sweep
below to keep the flow going, then push it out a lower door
for hauling away to market. Sometimes the corn is so deep —

unstable and crusted with age — that workers who are called inside
to walk it down off the sides, or poke it with a rod, are swept
into a crushing, whirl-pooling darkness, as if by flood, or rip
tide. A body's descent there is lonely, swift
. I read about a boy, 14, who was buried in a column
of 500,000 bushels, in the time it takes to read this poem.

/////

In 1993 an extraordinary opportunity to engage in landscape-scale restoration presented itself when the Department of Defense decided to decommission the 23,500-acre Joliet Army Arsenal. Built in the early years of World War II, the arsenal produced, at its peak, 5.5 million tons of TNT a week . . . . In the end, the land was transferred to the U.S. Forest Service to become the first National Tallgrass Prairie. Renamed Midewin National Tallgrass Prairie, the reserve currently holds fifteen thousand acres but has the potential of growing to 19,165 acres.

— Joel Greenberg, *A Natural History of the Chicago Region*

*The field draws
hawks and sides
of trains . . . .*

— Leila Wilson, "What is a Field?"

I never did find #63-1, the one bunker open
to the public. It wasn't where it was supposed

to be, at least according to free trail map
I picked up from the Midewin National

Tallgrass Prairie Welcome Center. It was
labeled a "Point of Interest" just past the Iron

Bridge, not far from the Explosives Road
Trailhead, and on the way to the main attraction,

the Bunker Field. Still, on that late June
morning, I went where the mowed trail led me,

crossing from the South Patrol Road Restoration
Area (which abutted the parking lot, where I'd left

Shiva in the car) to the River Road Seedbeds
and Turtle Pond, located not too far from the Prairie

Creek and South Arsenal Road, and walking on
to what the map showed as access to the Wauponsee

Glacial Trail, but based on these coordinates, I wasn't
sure what I was seeing. Was it restoration, or

decay? How to distinguish what might be remains
of a burial mound from a bunker masked by new

prairie grass? When does injury become repair?
The Bison Pastures designated nearby happened

to be closed, but just ahead where the trail
seemed to end, I couldn't miss a bull, enormous

even from that distance. I could make out his great
shaggy coat, how it had shed off in ragged

patches, exposing his leathery skin. He grazed
alone, inside a barbed wire fence.

Some accounts say
around the time Columbus arrived
there may have been bison herds of 40 to 60
million ranging freely across North America.

Some accounts say
what remains of the prairie
in what is now Illinois was formed
thousands of years ago, when the Wisconsin Ice
Sheet retreated north, and still, even 200 years ago
there were 21 million acres of prairie in Illinois,
though now, less than $\frac{1}{100}^{\text{th}}$ of 1% of it remains.

Some accounts say
it was 1830 when the first
white settler in the area, Charles Reed,
bought 162 acres of then undisturbed prairie
south of Joliet, Illinois, 40 or so miles south of Chicago,
from the US government, and 100 years later, that same federal
body bought back that same land — and the land of 149 other settlers —
to build a munitions plant.

Some accounts say
the area — 23,500 acres
established in 1939 — eventually
included 200 miles of roads, 166 miles
of railroads, 37 miles of 8-foot chain-link fencing
(with 3 strands of barbed wire) and 392 bunkers: remnants
now, each is 60 x 20 feet, with patterns on the walls left by the reinforced
concrete construction that formed the appearance of blocks
piled one on top of the other (for this shape
they were also known as "igloos") and used
mostly to store ammunition, explosives.

. . . accounts say
the Potawatomi nation cared for
other Chicago-area prairies until the 1830s,
when they were displaced by west-moving
white settlers, who were themselves displaced a century later.

. . . accounts say
hedgerow fences of Osage
orange trees still reach across
the trails, reminders of former farmers'
fields, just as tilting stone grave markers
in the few family burial plots left behind hold
the names of pioneers while the surrounding earth
holds the silenced generations of Civil War veterans,
and the more distant native tribes.

. . . accounts say
the 3 natural creeks that once
meanderingly crisscrossed the area
were channelized significantly to make straight the way
for bridge crossings, culverts, weirs, rip-rap, roads, drain tiles, dams.

. . . say
to complete the Joliet Army Arsenal
Plant (JOAAP), 45% of the landscape was modified
with over 1,000 of the total 1,462 buildings dating
back to WWII.

. . . say
the production of TNT
at its height reached 50 tons
per day — or every week the explosive equal
of 290 atomic bombs, similar to the one dropped
on Hiroshima — and the contaminants,
dumped daily into the creeks,
made them run red.

. . . say
late in WWII, available labor
was scarce so numbers of immigrants
from Barbados and Jamaica worked at the plant
and lived in segregated, so to speak, housing
on the grounds.

... say
at its peak, 10,425 people
were employed by JOAAP, though
others say it was closer to 18,000.

... say
in 1942, 28% of workers were women
and by summer 1944, 700 of them were
packing TNT — one worker was quoted as saying
assembling bombs and shells was like
*putting sugar in a bag, except you
have to be more careful.*

... say
originally there were 2 plants:
Elwood Ordnance and Kankakee Ordnance Works
and construction costs for them was $81 million: Kankakee
(which some say comes from the Miami-Illinois word
teeyaahkiki meaning "open country/land in the open")
set a national record for the time, producing 1
billion pounds of TNT, and while not a record,
Elwood loaded over 926 million bombs.

... say
after WWII the plant
was placed on standby,
and sure enough was later
reactivated during the Korean War
and the Vietnam War, though early in
the 1990s, it was decommissioned.

. . . say
plans for future uses
of the arsenal lands went beyond
restoring prairie: industrial parks, a landfill,
the Abraham Lincoln National Cemetery.

There are 5 types
of bunkers: weapons,
industrial, artillery, trench, personal.

Some of the abandoned
JOAPP bunkers are now being used
for storing seeds of indigenous plants.

Other bunkers at retired
munitions depots around the US are
being repurposed as luxury doomsday
condos, complete with movie theatres, bowling alleys,
grocery stores, dog parks, conference rooms, video
game arcades, bullet-resistant doors,
gun ranges.

In the mid-1940s,
in the US, JOAAP was just
1 of 77 other arsenals across the land
like it.

Fishes and crayfishes indigenous
to the area and thought lost forever—like
the Gizzard Shad, Common Stoneroller, Striped Shiner,
Red Shiner, Hornyhead Chub, Bigmouth Shiner, Roseyface Shiner,
Southern Redbelly Dace, Bluntnose Minnow, White Sucker, Golden Redhorse,
Black Bullhead, Yellow Bullhead, Slender Madtom, Warmouth, Bluegill,
Largemouth Bass, Fantail Darter, Johnny Darter, Black Buffalo, Devil
Crayfish, River Crayfish, Northern Crayfish,
Prairie Crayfish—are beginning to return.

Some accounts
say "Midewin"
is *the* Potawatomi
word for healing, and
others say it is *a* Potawatomi
word for healing.

On this midwestern landscape, I was
surrounded by the bare bones of preparation
for three wars: World War II, the Korean
War, and the Vietnam War. I stood there
first in February 1995.

— Terry Evans, photographer, from
Disarming the Prairie (1998), a compilation of
her photos of former Joliet Army Arsenal site.

Given the vastness of it all, many of Evans' photos are aerial,
taken from a yellow Piper Cub plane at an altitude of 700 feet,
and record what appears to be a zigzagging of seams, more like

suturings, as if some great excised body had been left on this
scarred and re-scarred landscape and marred by the leavings
of so many hurried, warfaring surgeries and post-ops gone

terribly awry: empty barracks, drained pump stations, tilting
weapons warehouses, power lines undone, askew, abandoned
trains left in and at the edges of corn fields, some at still-open

bunker doors, manufacturing vats full of shadows, manhole
covers necklaced by weeds, natural gas pipelines unlined, wall-
less office buildings, furnace buildings, guard houses and gates,

a weathered fire station, aboveground magazines squatting in
alternating lines across the east boundary, and the now near invisible
burning grounds for explosives, marked only by a length of bent

metal fencing and a faded sign reading   X - *LOSIVES*
BURNING GROUNDS. Still, her book has the quality of a weaving —
the sturdy, mostly upright warp of the arsenal imagery held

in tension with the weft of time and histories and the transverse
rhythms of a remnant prairie: wetland   red-winged blackbird
  nest   tangle of dropseed grass   jawbone of a deer.

The burying, the
buried, to bury: hide, al-
so to immerse, save.

In Livingston County, just a few miles southeast of Will County, where the Midewin National Tallgrass Prairie is now being restored, a botanist, scholar of Illinois natural history, sets up his Plantograph, a tool he developed himself for this study of one plot of rare, high quality, old-growth prairie: a small platform to support him, his camera, hat, jacket, knapsack, and measuring devices so that he can determine, painstakingly and to the nearest millimeter, each plant present—stem, cluster of basal leaves, seedling—in this precisely drawn 20x20-inch square. Monitoring it all throughout this growing season, he'll then return at regular intervals going forward, to begin learning how this ancient, unplowed, ungrazed prairie got itself to this density, self-possession. At the outset, he notes 551 stems of 30 native species (+ 1 invasive: *Poa pratensis* :: Kentucky Bluegrass):

Amorpha canescens :: Lead Plant

Andropogon gerardii :: Big Bluestem

Carex bicknellii :: Bicknell's Sedge

Carex meadii :: Mead's Sedge   *Comandra umbellata* :: False Toadflax

Coreopsis palmata :: Prairie Coreopsis

Dichanthelium leibergii :: Prairie Panic Grass

Eryngium yuccifolium :: Rattlesnake Master

Euphorbia corollata :: Flowering Spurge

Gentiana puberulenta :: Prairie Gentian

Helianthus pauciflorus :: Stiff Sunflower

Hesperostipa spartea :: Porcupine Grass

Lactuca canadensis :: Canada Wild Lettuce

Liatris aspera :: Rough Blazing Star

Nabalus racemosus :: Smooth Prairie Lettuce

Oxalis violacea :: Violet Wood Sorrel

Pedicularis canadensis :: Prairie Lousewort

Phlox pilosa :: Prairie Phlox

Physalis virginiana :: Prairie Ground Cherry

Physostegia virginiana :: Obedient Plant   *Poa pratensis* :: Kentucky Bluegrass

Ratibida pinnata :: Yellow Coneflower

Rosa carolina :: Carolina Rose   *Rudbeckia hirta* :: Black-eyed Susan

Silphium integrifolium :: Rosinweed

Silphium laciniatum :: Compass Plant   *Silphium terebinthinaceum* :: Prairie Dock

Symphyotrichum oolentangiense :: Sky-blue Aster

Tradescantia ohiensis :: Ohio Spiderwort

Parthenium integrifolium :: Feverfew

Schizachyrium scoparium :: Little Bluestem

What is the distance,
difference between

burying the dead
and burying what killed

the dead when the killing
is carried in the root

systems, the water
tables, the red creeks, the

railroad bed runoff, the fickle
resulting moods of climate

changes incised on every surface,
through each understory,

species, tribe, family, the detritus
only faintly lost to the naked

eye? As I write
this, I recall you

increasingly buried
in me — seeming like

ages ago, when you were
dying. So I'm (re)writing —

a patchwork, seams, despite
tears, these tears.

Remnant Lament

O n c e a b u n d a n c e
O n c e abundance
Once abundance.
Once, abundance.
Once, [a]bundance.
Once, [b]undance
Once, [u]ndance.
Once, [n]dance.
Once, [d]ance.
Once, [a]nce.
Once, [n]ce.
Once, [c]e.
Once, [e].
Once,

,

Dear Prairie, I've been meaning

to ….   Ever since I can remember, you …
I still keep it, that old photo: me, my … ,
brothers, father …. All those years traveling
back through you, I …. Looking out the car
window, I saw your … , vastness …. I wanted
 … you to know … even though I was
small, voiceless, … less …. I now carry
your … gold, … grasses … a rhythm. I have
tried to … but only remnants, a fading I
know …. A chance to repair … re-
pair …. A needle's eye, this … I am
learning to read … stay … awake. If
 … get this … write …

/////

II. A Mending

And this is the only way to tell if a soil
Is rich or not: when you work it with your hands

— Virgil, *The Georgics*

lyre lyre lyre

transparent dress

— Sappho

New Medium

I'm learning to write my name
with thread, drawn through the eye
of a fine new needle, held in place by
its shank above the silver throat plate

of my Singer. I listen for the balance
wheel to engage, as I press — easy now —
the treadle, and steadying with my hands
a remnant of your worn blue shirt (how

long since you've been gone?) I remember
            the way your body moved under it so
easily when we walked, the late September
light writing itself across your back, no

tension, snags. Slowly, I sew *M-a-r*, try
to master the how of this, before finishing the *y*.

Underground Fence

I'd never heard of it until
then, until after you were
gone, and everything seemed to be
suddenly leaking, or breaking,
or gaping. It was as if all the walls wore
themselves to shredding holes overnight,
while the light bulb filaments lit up
like tiny off-season sparklers before
going out. I thought I felt winsome
breezes weaving a chill through the living
room, and when I saw a flash of white
in the backyard at dusk, I never told anyone
that I thought it was a fleeting remnant
of you, the physics of your vanishing. It turned
out to be a skunk, a descendent no doubt
of those who'd made themselves known
through each of our hapless dogs.
But I hadn't seen how intrepid
they are, digging and digging under
the foundation, snouts pressing toward
any nesting place. No placement over time
of stones or bricks deterred, so I
hired experts to install the underground
fence that now, years later, has kept
anything from getting to me.

Widow with Extra Doors

It started with the hospital bed, its odd longness, as if it knew
something about what lay ahead, and all those curious projections —
springs, gears, levers, a red button coiled for the touch
with power for the uprising, or down-curving of the body —
like custom-made hooks to hang the gear on we didn't even know
we'd be needing, as if it were already adjusted for the passage, the inexorable
already emptiness, but also the also already ahead too. There was no way to fit it all in
our bedroom without some kind of removal — stripping it down,
or taking off the door. So I tapped the heavy
hinges with a tack hammer, surprised at how easily each lifted from its rust, too
fast, too fast it seemed to me. What was the point then
in keeping the other doors attached — they just seemed so useless, letting in
all that they had. I went about unhinging
three more up there, carrying them awkwardly down to our unfinished
basement, where they still are, going
nowhere. I'm a little remorseful I didn't go there
sooner — maybe we could have found a way. Anyway,
who knew how big the gap in all this light would be.

With Shims

As if you could be
enticed to return by
my effort, embodied,
to turn back the bed, to
beckon what once was
there, again, as if my repainting, re-
touching, paying attention
to lines, to naming
colors for these empty surfaces —
Atmospheric, Distant Thunder,
Wandering Heart — might undo
what is done, how I have now
begun the rest of my life shoring
up, trueing, trying
to set my listing horizon
straight, one thin shim
at a time.

Left with Pawpaw Tree

You had read ahead,
as usual, in the life cycle,

learned the limits
of the pawpaw, how

(the phone rings as I write, the answering
machine, I hear a disembodied voice, another
call for you)

despite the perfect design — both
male and female reproductive parts

present — there's nonetheless no self-
pollination. You made

those trips across town from the Arboretum
to home, a Q-tip tipped with pollen from one

there, for ours here, where your touch made
possible what I found this fall I'm sure

for the last time: the fruit
of you, your labors.

The Garden Bed

The garden bed I put to bed
looked, once I'd covered it over
and over, like a grave, with the detritus of that
last season, mostly leavings' leathery skeletons,
a bric-a-brac from the backyard, your
hub, your habitat, the same one near where you spent
your end, the long limbs of your life nonetheless still
almost opening with bright green buds of who
knows what, even the nimbus of your final
breaths, a kind of soughing, sewing, I
thought you were just sleeping in
that early fall haze, pollens having
done their delving, all
the making made.

Möebius

I'll try again to begin the end,
a poem to finally face your agonal
passage — that mad möebius rend
before the hellified path to null —

the never-coming-back slackness
of death, setting on like a worn glove
over your beautiful, vanishing face.
If I hadn't seen it for myself, Love,

I wouldn't have believed how
irretrievable, how already were
      you were.
I'm not sure what there is to now,

or if there's any point in trying again,
and again, and again, to begin the end.

With the Unworn

While shifting the weight
of winter, from one wardrobe
to another, I came across
them, those odd embodiments we

bought before a journey we never got to take
to some remote, unspoiled islands off
the Pacific coast, weren't we hoping to keep
the salty cold out, at bay that swift

stiffening of limbs, how do they
say it, *in extremis*? How I had hung
them up there, oh, I'd been meaning
to give them away, body-like

un-bodied spectres, black, rubbery,
tags still on, promising to insulate through
the slightest permeability, just enough getting in
for the body to heat it — cinched synthetic

layers and blind-stitched seams taped,
taped again — against seepings, dark
pressures, though of course,
all the while, letting
them in.

Referred Pain

Worrying about Shiva took me
that week to a place of steep dis-
traction, amplified by the persistent
autumnal rain, a certain kind

of prisming — for me a slowing,
splitting, soft piercing. Knowing
there was something wrong with her,
it was hard to be present to anything

but what I couldn't know. Turned out
she had an inflammation somewhere
in her leg, neck, spine, a small spiking
chain of referred pain. The vet's meds

worked swiftly, and in the midst
of her transformation back to her-
self, I realized suddenly I was likely
the cause of it all, my pulling and

yanking her hard by her leash, harsh
hurrying commands too, even, even
on our short walks, fierce, unyielding
in my impatience with her deliberation

over a tiny leaf, or stone, her long pausing
to take in what, in my own blinding
grief, was invisible to me.

Sugaring for Moths

The filmy shapes that haunt the dusk.

— Tennyson, "In Memoriam A.H.H."

Whatever fruit is on hand, mash with wine or beer
in a slurry, add a couple cups of sugar, white or brown,
a shot of rum, dollop of molasses, or maple syrup.

To a cheap bottle of white wine, add 2-3 spoons of sugar,
shake, let sit, the longer the better but ok to use the same
night. Cut a piece of clothesline (anchor rope is ok), dip

both ends in wine bottle. Hang rope over a limb so both ends
are dangling. Best time at dusk. Dip the ropes back into
the wine nightly, though some come without re-dipping.

One can of beer (or apple cider), 1½ cups sugar, ¼-½ cup
molasses, about four over-ripe bananas or equivalent in
apples, peaches, pears, quinces, etc., a brewer's yeast tablet

(optional), and a spoonful of cornmeal (optional). Mix
in blender, allow to ferment in warm slightly vented jar
for a few days. Good bait will smell strongly of alcohol.

Paint on trees with a brush just before dark. Then search
after dark with light to see if they have returned to you
from the thicket. If necessary, repeat in memoriam.

/////

Then again,

       my heart might be a prairie,

its distant beating, waves
from an ancient inland

sea, traveling in tallgrass
songs of seed, bird, bone, weather,

shadows trapped in loam, hands
of ancestors, their ghost maps

pressing into sod, made
to stand despite the unbroken

wind, vanishings,
            loneliness

Woven Field

— *after* And Water Meets Sky, *miniature
weaving (9½ x 4½ in.): cotton, silk,
reversible, all selvages finished.
Sheila Hicks, b. 1934, Hastings, Nebraska*

Held in vertical filaments of celestial blue silk,
Sheila Hicks' key thoughts extend the reversible
subject of her weaving: a blurring convergence
of sea, sky, her artist's eye. Drawn up and down,
these warp threads suggest sky, land. Anyone can see
she uses a small loom, miniature world view (no less

true) to move past, and in toward her mind. Beyond
this, she takes up the horizon, a back-and-forth tanglement
thickening space into pattern, or if she pleases, opening
into slits, slots, the swervings of weft. Here again sea-
sky blue, but now pearl gray, green cotton too. What moves
me is the pale yellow, almost hay, hint of Hicks' Midwest
roots, prairies: bluestem, blazing star, inland salt, cord grass
oceans' wavering, and all captured in this small woven field.

Underworld

Without you now, again I come here
for the weave, a slow tangling together and
apart of birdsong, wind, sky,

and the underworld, miles
and miles of roots that have,
in other now remnants of what

once was, been cut and parsed,
split into parcels that fall
back, and sometimes again back

into the earth where everything
belongs, but that here, in the Flint Hills,
could not be severed, its skull cap

of chert, which has for millennia
made plowing, furrowing, building un-
wise, and so I come here

for aimlessness, for
the loneliness of spontaneity
unshared, for vastness on this

grand old bone of the land and I
admit it, yes, to un-map myself
and our million maps that I keep

carrying, like there would be some-
where to go, and all I have been
able to find is how slow I am, failed

carpenter gazing into the still unrepaired
and gaping hole, day after day, year after
year, blown in me by your vanishing, vaster

than this sky, and for example,
it wasn't until I lost
for the third time Shiva's

leash — she and I'd been way, way, way, way, way
out on some open range road, tracing,
because we could, cloud-lines

across the highest rim of
the hill, and seeing clear to the next
where three wild horses might be

standing, as if in a Western,
their tails and manes blowing like
the end of the story was close, and then

we, Shiva and me, walking
back, and when I reached
for the leash, found it gone, itself

unleashed, a leather strand, not at all not
at home on the open range where it could have
originated, pelt, sinew, somehow, another

element close to this prairie, and returning way, way, way
out there I found it the next day,
which didn't stop me from losing it

out there again, and again, and
then, the last time, as if shedding
a skin, or cutting

a line, I left it.

Flint Hills, Konza Prairie, Kansas: Five-Year Mark

This time back, by chance, I can see
the brown-spotted, narrower end
of a cowbird egg, resting broken
open, under a blooming catalpa, free

from its confinements: earlier,
whole inside the small female's body,
then later, quickly laid, left cunningly
to crowd eggs out of the nest of another,

any species — warbler, vireo, blackbird.
Five years ago, I'd have easily despaired
of the cruel but clever cowbird, skilled brood
parasite, while holding my own self-pity bare.

But this time, I also see a tiny cup, in shadows,
fine porcelain, or bone, full to half with dew.

Hardly

1. Untamed

O tousled hair

— Rimbaud

Hardly
a night goes

by
when I

don't wake
from it, its

core,
missing

you back
next to me

your untamed
black hair

2. Fade

I've wondered,
wandering

in the Konza
Prairie, where you

your remains are
now,

scattered
as they were

by my trembling
hands, so

long
ago, now

3. Before this

Unlike you,
perennial,

everything
now   goes

    :   like this
moment, or this light

field fog emerging
as quickly as

it recedes —
unveiling what is

left: the common
milkweed, husks of

scaly blazing stars,
brush heaps

4. Being Built

I am living in the house being built
when I saw you last — and inch by inch
it is becoming — my house — something
that feels like my shell to live in . . .

— Georgia O'Keeffe

I know now
that I didn't know

then, when
we were

still we, I
was

already
building

my next
be-

com-
ing

5. Burning the Grass

The last
walk

we took
together

on the prairie, there
was a fire, pre-

scribed to burn
away the last

of the last year's
grass, making way for

the new. Wasn't it
everywhere in us?

And

Strand of wild horse hair
snagged in a fence barb — prairie
wind writes its absence.

/////

Palimpsest

As in writing, as in memory, as in shelter, as in
delineations of form, say, the living

walls of a sod house, the corporeal, the body of,
(you) begin with

a surface, plain, skin, supple, tough — buffalo, cow,
deer — respectfully, respect-

fully removed, scraped of fur on one side, and
from the other textures,

membranes, sinews of muscle, all the attachments
of the living and

then, the washing, the stretching, the intimacies
of softening, before and

then the drying, the rubbing, smoothing, then the
cutting into shape, into

desire: scribe, incise, a text for holding until another,
other, author, scribe, a search

for surface displaces, finds a place for the mind, story,
map, idea, scripture, all

over again scrape, rescribe, rub, rub   smooth, scrape, un-
bind, refold, leaving

always, all ways the shadows of the written over, of what
was, is, scraped now, rubbed

again, rubbed again   smoothed by hand, by time, by
method, moods of sovereignty,

acquisition, appropriation, denial, the contested
histories of   what preceded

and what overtakes, over-
powers, overscrapes, intentionally

or not, from scarcity, or not, now rub   rub   again
smooth.   Again, to be

rubbed   smoothed by time, an undoing of, say, something
ancient, a world, like Archimedes'

incomparable proofs that he wrote in Sicily, in Greek,
3rd century BC, and addressed as

letters to his contemporaries — on buoyancy, the nature and
form and gravity of floating

bodies, and also on the use of indivisibles and exhaustion
as modes for inquiry, and

more — and all this eventually lost, then found, then
copied, but lost again in that safe-

keeping way, turning up in another country, after some
sacking, and in a monastery

where, they were, by a monk, unbound, scraped, washed, then
reshaped, refolded, and re-

used for a liturgical tract, some 177 pages, and by then
it was 1269. Now,

having somehow survived generations, more sackings, wars,
forgeries, and the careless

overwritings, stashings, damagings from water and mold,
they've been unlayered, made

available to all, those long-lost, layered-over brilliancies
from that ancient, crystalline

mind, that old math emerging new through
varieties of light, literacy.

Unravelment

— after Dégringolade, *weaving by Sheila Hicks, and her comment: "A raucous character — wiggling to an uncertain destiny — collapses in broad daylight, completely undone. I abandoned this small work only to retrieve it twenty years later with new interest." Woven, floating warp; cotton, silk (8⅝ x 6¾ in.)*

Tumble collapse it's hard to read this weaving's
gradual unravelment how the steady gold warp goes
soon loses its grip the weft drifting loose left to bundle
slip run colors askew a single-strand mauve silk giving
way to slubby worsteds rust and navy green grey while
a thin snarl of undone maroon threads tangle a patch
remnant dangling ajar orphan does it still belong or want
to drift the fraying river like tresses for mourning repair

even the word tumbles *dégringolade* like a full shuttle
traveling across over under almost all the vowel threads
while bumping up back and forth against a couple of hard-
knock consonants those *d*'s, those *g*'s just a nudge then
a rest on the *n* of *in* the *l* of *la* like loess it's flux forever
in a state of undone completely raucous uncertain destiny

Somehow Forgotten

During the distant reign
of King Khufu, famed as builder
of the Great Pyramid on the Giza Plateau,
between 2551 and 2528 B.C., somewhere

nearby, a woman of some means died.
Mummified and buried with a beadnet dress
perhaps sewn on or simply draped over her
form, this was fine geometry, a wide even

collar, fringed with gold floral pendants
floating above the bodice and its echoing
skirt of blue and blue-green cylinder faience
beads — suggesting lapis lazuli, turquoise —

strung on the merest thread disappearing
around the contours of her torso, which thus
became what once must have been a glorious
scrim over her body, 7,000 of these tiny pierced

orbs found when her undisturbed tomb
was opened in 1927 by an excavation team.
In the black and white photo they took,
tonal shadows showed bones untethered

by time from the somber linen wrapping,
the once hot resin's hold, but held nonetheless
in that peace that must come, that contemplation
held lightly, reverently, in silence, by scatterings

and scatterings of these beads, mostly in random
heaps along her spine, or accidental alignments
at her elbow, or shoulder. But a few, settling
on her wide pelvic bones, offered a recognizable

enough pattern. Scholar Millicent Jick had studied
paintings of women in waiting on walls of Egyptian
tombs, how their bodies moved in friezes, their
garments shaping and freeing. When she found

the beadnet mummy in the museum basement,
somehow forgotten, she set to restringing using
ladder and diamond net stitches, and after months
restored the diaphanous original, not one bead left over.

Scaffolding

*Cardiac scientist Doris Taylor and her team
garnered international recognition in 2008 for
work showing they were able to remove existing
cells from hearts of lab animals and even humans
leaving a framework to build new organs.*

Translucent globe of a thing I saw you
hold in your hand in the video, Doris, you were
in your lab explaining how from a once-
beating heart you washed every cell,
a delicate scrubbing with soap that left this
scaffolding of collagen empty, pale, but marked
with the intricate vessels and chambers,
even the holes for holding valves, a light
map of what life had once been there, you
pointed out these tracings, turning the heart
over and gently again over in the palm
of your hand, and you said there was enough
memory in this cardiac architecture, so that
when stem cells were injected there,
by the millions, by you, along with
an electrical signal, the necessary
mechanical blood pressure, and oxygen,
there was, approximately 8 days later,
a beat. Ghost heart is what you called it.

Am I

     a dovecote
now   full with holes

to make   to hold
    a place for the fleeing,   for the flight

    from somewhere to here   or
    from here to that no-

where for those   bereft
    of being

    loved   by the beloved
      who has flown   alone

to a where
       where

        there is
no coming back from   ever?

Absent Presence: Triptych

Textiles remember.

— Jessica Hemmings

When at last I opened

How vast it all seemed — with you gone — the ghostly
shapes that shifted when at last I opened your closet,
then quick, closed it again, your still-clear presence

too clear, too near. It took months for your presence
to drift, or lift into some other place, less ghostly
than I could see, then. I remembered my mother's closet

those many years before, where I found her closest,
even years after she'd vanished, having left so many presents —
blouses, suits, dresses, coats, stoles — to open, a ghostly

ghosting. Her closet, like yours now, an absent presence.

I am opening. Seams

Before piecing this quilt, I read marks left by your work
in the folds, the fraying shadows of your blue jeans,
which now, so much later, I am opening. Seams

I split with the tiny curved blade of my ripper seem
like lines a writer might conjure, then revise to rework
as a life to fit a life. Textile maps, stitch trails — your jeans:

hems, inseams, waists, belt keepers, pockets. Your jeans
bear tracings of your gait, your leanings, the seaming
drawn by the curve of your hips, how you knelt to work

in the garden. Your work, I now unwork, your jeans unseam.

of you — faded, fading

Hadn't I known that too, too soon this now
would come? When the best I saved for last
of you — faded, fading work clothes you left

behind, suddenly — would be all the fabric I've left
of you? A pile of worn blue jeans, unworn by now
years, years. Not nearly enough to fend off the last

of it — the inevitable end, the using up of, the last
word. No piecing you, your remnants, your left-
behind scatterings brings you here to mend this now.

So now's here, at last, and all that's left.

Note to a Hingeless Coral Pink Door Floating in the Woods

— After An Anecdote, *by Joe Wight*
Old Frog Pond Farm & Studio
Outdoor Sculpture Exhibit, 2019
Harvard, Massachusetts

You took my breath away
when I first saw you suspended
in the trees like a story unhinged

from its time, place, its meanings
opening then shifting with each passer-
by, narrator. You appeared to me

to be a door, but knobless, hinge-
less, homeless (not even a lintel
disrupted your maverick pink coral

character) you suggested another
theme, as did your effortless floating,
so poised, unencumbered. I wanted

you to know I've taken you to heart,
my heart, in particular, too long hinged to loss
and longing for something like you.

Late in the Season, Widow Gardening

First, though, to determine what must go —
fading dianthus, silvering thistle, and the end of a bee
balm bloom, the ragged crown's last glow.

Pruning, next, a taking that knows
pressure, where the blade should kiss, cleave,
to undo what was, make way for the slow, low

new growth. How does it always know
about opening there, where nothing is, despite grief
fuller than all those fragments by Sappho?

*

Fuller than all those fragments by Sappho
about opening there, where nothing is, despite grief,
new growth. How does it always know

to undo what was, make way for thc slow, low
pressure, where the blade should kiss, cleave?
Pruning, next, a taking that knows

balm, bloom, the ragged crown's last glow —
a fading dianthus, silvering thistle, and the end of a bee.
First, though, to determine what must go.

/////

Zizia aptera,

yellow-gold
extraordinarily
whimsical wildflower, a little whirligigish,
vulnerable (with your heart-shaped
undivided leaves) and those umbels that hold
tender clusters of tiny flowers, within tinier flowers,
still, and again, within even tinier flowers, whorls, worlds,
tight, your delicate
rosettes,
quilted, or embroidered so
precisely are you stitched in the heart of the prairie,
ornate with you, especially in early May.

Numb from missing what once must have been,
my heart
lingers over how you
keep in your keep
just what you can, leaving your
inscription.

Here, close to
ground, when I can
find you, I know I'm finding someone
else, remains of remains, regardless of
drought, or trampling, or
cycles unwound, you are a taproot to
bedrock,
all.

Notes

All references to Sheila Hicks' weavings, and accompanying commentaries, are taken with permission from *Sheila Hicks: Weaving as Metaphor*, published for The Bard Graduate Center for Studies in the Decorative Arts, Design and Culture, New York, by Yale University Press, New Haven and London, 2006.

Sources for "Some accounts say" include:

Greenberg, Joel. *A Natural History of the Chicago Region.* Chicago: University of Chicago Press, 2002: 469-470.

Jeffords, Michael and Susan Post, eds. *Exploring Nature in Illinois: A Field Guide to the Prairie State.* Urbana, IL: University of Illinois Press, 2014.

National Forest Foundation: *Midewin National Tallgrass Prairie: A Shared Vision for Restoration.* www.nationalforest.org

Thoel, Sean. "From TNT to Tallgrass: Prairie Restoration at a Munitions Plant Turned National Grassland." *Edge Effects.* Madison, WI: Center for Culture, History, and Environment, University of Wisconsin-Madison: July 11, 2017.

USDA Forest Service: Midewin National Tallgrass Prairie. www.fs.usda.gov/midewin

The epigraphs from Virgil are taken from *The Georgics of Virgil* (Farrar, Straus and Giroux, 2005), translated by David Ferry.

Acknowledgments

Grateful acknowledgment is made to the following journals and publications in which the following poems first appeared:

"Late in the Season, Widow Gardening," honorable mention in the Tor House Prize for Poetry 2017. www.torhouse.org/prize

"Note to a Hingeless Coral Pink Door Floating in the Woods," *Speaking of Sculpture: Ekphrastic Poetry & Outdoor Sculpture.*

"Palimpsest," *Ecotone 32 (Spring/Summer 2022).*

"So when I saw for the first time," *Moving Images: Poetry Inspired by Cinema.*

"Somehow Forgotten," *Southern Poetry Review.*

"Underground Fence," *Poem of the Moment, Mass Poetry.*

"Widow Sugaring for Moths," *Salamander.*

"Widow with Extra Doors," *Nimrod International Journal.*

I extend my deep gratitude to Patty and Jerry Reece, dear friends and owners of The Volland Store just outside Alma, Kansas, which features a Residency Program for artists and writers. I wrote many of the poems in *Ghost Heart* there. In addition, I express my appreciation to the Babson College Faculty Research Fund for grant support, which made my travels to Kansas possible.

I also owe enormous thanks to the following — friends, mentors, readers, artists — who have offered me their wisdom, example, and abiding support: Jennifer Barber, Elizabeth Dodd, David Ferry, Kathleen Flenniken, Brandi George, Sheila Hicks, Alice Huffman, Moira Linehan, Carolyn Megan, Mary O'Donoghue, Estelle Travers Smith, Melanie Rae Thon, Wendy Thon, and my families in Seattle, Kansas, and New York. And to Miles, most of all.

About the Author

Mary Pinard teaches in the Arts & Humanities Division at Babson College in Wellesley, MA. Her first collection of poems, *Portal*, was published by Salmon Press in 2014. Her poems have appeared in *Prairie Schooner, Iowa Review, Georgia Review, Southern Poetry Review, Boston Review,* and *Salamander*, among others. She has also created poems in collaboration with Boston-area musicians, painters, and sculptors. She was born and raised in Seattle.

Colophon

Printed by Bookmobile in Minneapolis, Minnesota, on Boise 70-lb. offset white paper. The text and titles are set in Minion Pro.